DEDICATED TO ALL THE GRANDCHILDREN

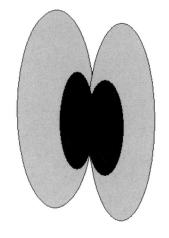

ACKNOWLEDGEMENTS

A SOUTH CAROLINA CHRONOLOGY 1497-1992 SECOND EDITION for the historical accuracy.

THE WRITERS GROUP at BARNES AND NOBLE for their excellent suggestions and input.

MARY NEFF for getting Carol and I together and for writing the bio-text on Carol.

THE CIVIL WAR by KEN BURNS for photo inspiration.

BETTY ROSENLIEB for her inspiration and putting up with the insanity.

MY FAMILY, for their help, support, and encouragement.

THE CITY OF CHARLESTON, for keeping things the way they are.

To Ms. Sherbine
and her 2nd Grader Class
Always be Looking + Listening!

Thanks,

Jeff C. Williams
11-22-08

A MUD'S EYE VIEW OF CHARLESTON'S HISTORY

BY
JOSEPH C. WILSON

PAINTINGS BY
CAROL ANN POWELL

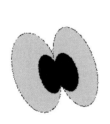

PUBLISHED BY

JOSEPH C. WILSON DBA

MUDDUDS

CHARLESTON, SOUTH CAROLINA

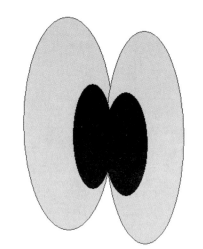

Hey, how are ya? My name is PLUFFER and I'm the gray, greenish brown, sticky ooze they call PLUFF MUD here in CHARLESTON.

You know, CHARLESTON, SOUTH CAROLINA, where the ASHLEY and COOPER RIVERS meet to form the ATLANTIC OCEAN.

Charleston is located in an area that is often referred to as THE LOW COUNTRY because the land is so close to sea level and flat for as far as my eyes can see. I've heard about mountains, but I still haven't seen anything that looks like one over in MOUNT PLEASANT.

I can look very different depending on what is happening with the TIDES. When the tide is HIGH, I'm covered by water and get to be with all my underwater friends. I know all the FISH, SHRIMP, CRABS, and OYSTERS. They depend on me for food and shelter. I've heard that I'm a very important part of something called an ECO SYSTEM.

You can see me and many of my underwater friends at the SOUTH CAROLINA AQUARIUM.
The people there will be happy to explain this ECO SYSTEM, and tell you all about life under the water.

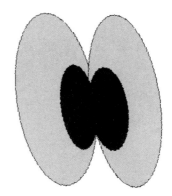

While things under the water haven't changed very much, that's not true for the land above the water. Oh, the stories I can tell, but I'm getting ahead of myself.

You see, when the tide is LOW, I become part of the land and I can SEE and HEAR EVERYTHING, and have I ever SEEN and HEARD A LOT.

Let's see now, the changes really started many tides ago when I saw this HUGE LOG float in at high tide.

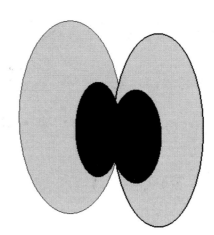

At low tide, I discovered that it wasn't a log at all! It was the BIGGEST BOAT I had ever seen, and on it was a whole village of people. They wore strange clothes and didn't speak like my Indian friends.

It seems they had traveled a long way from a place called ENGLAND and were very happy to finally see me.

They spoke often about a KING and that was the first time I ever saw something called a FLAG.

These people called themselves COLONISTS and built their homes and a church at a place that is now called CHARLES TOWNE LANDING. They planted many different crops, but found that RICE, INDIGO, COTTON, and TOBACCO grew the best.

I saw more boats arrive and farms started to spring up all over THE LOW COUNTRY. Eventually the village, now called CHARLES TOWN, moved to it's present location.

Soon, the farms became PLANTATIONS with names like DRAYTON HALL, MAGNOLIA, MIDDLETON PLACE, and BOONE HALL. The Plantations were very busy growing the crops and making the bricks and lumber that were needed as Charles Town grew.

Many of the people who worked in the fields and did the chores were called SLAVES. They worked very hard and spoke often of a place called AFRICA, but they didn't seem happy to be here.

Then one night, I remember hearing these four men talking about LIBERTY and FREEDOM from British Rule. They complained about the TAXES and said the KING was never going to be satisfied. It seems the British had even shot some of the COLONISTS in MASSACHUSETTS. They said they were going to a City called PHILADELPHIA to meet with other PATRIOTS and sign something called a DECLARATION OF INDEPENDENCE.

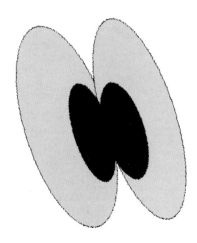

A few tides came and went and I saw these BRITISH ships shooting at Charles Town. They fought with the Colonists and even took over the city. Many battles were fought all over the Low Country.

Then one day, I saw a great looking new flag flying over FORT MOULTRIE. The flag had 13 star and 13 stripes, one for each of the 13 Colonies that were now called STATES. It seems I was part of a new country called the UNITED STATES of AMERICA!

As the AMERICANS celebrated their new Independence, the British and their friends took their Flag and sailed away.

Every so often I would notice that there was another Star on the Flag. The British even tried to come back, but the AMERICANS would have none of that.

I saw ships flying many different Flags arrive, in what was now CHARLESTON, with people and goods from all over the world and leave with what was produced on the Plantations. The ships were getting bigger and some didn't even have sails.

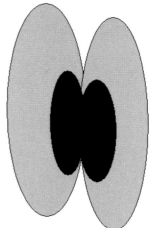

Then one day, when the Flag had 33 stars, I started
hearing talk about STATES RIGHTS. A man named
LINCOLN was running for PRESIDENT and if he was
elected, the people said they were going to SECEDE
from the UNION and form their own country called the
CONFEDERATE STATES of AMERICA..

Now, all the UNION soldiers used to wear blue,
but after LINCOLN was elected,
some of them started wearing gray.
They called themselves
CONFEDERATES and even had
their own new FLAG.

One night, I saw all the blue Union soldiers move everything they could out to FORT SUMTER. The Confederates kept asking them to leave, but the Union soldiers refused. A few tides passed, then early one morning the Confederates started shooting their cannons at the Fort.

Soon, FORT SUMTER was surrendered and the Union soldiers took down the Stars and Stripes and went back up North. This was the start of THE CIVIL WAR and it happened right here in Charleston!

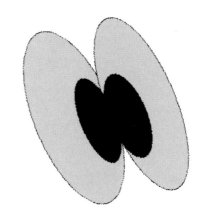

A few more tides came and went when I started to see UNION ships stationed just outside the harbor. I heard they were there to keep all the other ships away. It was called a BLOCKADE.

This blockade really hurt Charleston, so these real smart Confederates built a boat called the HUNLEY. Instead of just floating on the water like other boats, it could also move under the water like a fish. The HUNLEY did its best to help break

this blockade by sinking
the UNION ship HOUSATONIC
just before it also sank.

The blockade continued and, try as they did, the Confederate ships could not make the Union ships leave. Without the ships bringing in supplies, the people of Charleston suffered greatly.

More tides passed and one day I noticed that all the soldiers were once again wearing blue and the old STARS and STRIPES was flying over FORT SUMTER. The blockade was gone and the ships were again able to come and go. The SLAVES seemed much happier, now that they were FREE, and life for everyone was forever changed.

The people of Charleston began to rebuild their once beautiful city, always trying to preserve their heritage as well as the buildings. They made a special effort to restore the City to the way it was before the CIVIL WAR. They seemed to know, even then, that their HISTORY would be their FUTURE.

Since then, an EARTHQUAKE, a FIRE, and a few HURRICANES have tried to knock CHARLESTON down, but each time the City and its people came back better than before.

Every night, the MORRIS ISLAND LIGHTHOUSE would shine its beacon out to sea directing the ships to come to Charleston. I saw the Flag get even more stars and watched The Low Country grow.

I would hear the sailors talk about other wars in other places, but since the CIVIL WAR there hasn't been any real fighting here.

I sure am glad because those cannonballs REALLY HURT !!!

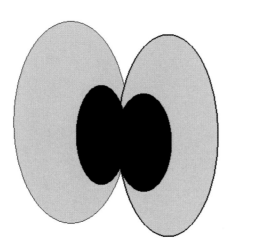

31

I don't see as many Navy ships as I once did, but there are still some over at PATRIOTS POINT in Mount Pleasant that you can visit. They were in those other wars and really have some great stories to tell.

The submarines today sure look different from the old HUNLEY. By the way, when you see the HUNLEY, tell it Pluffer said "Hey"! It used to hide under me until it was found a few tides ago.

We were good friends and I did my best to preserve it.

Today, a modern lighthouse on SULLIVAN'S ISLAND
beckons the ships to come to Charleston. I've heard it's one of the
biggest ports on the East Coast and those container and cruise
ships sure are bigger than the boat I mistook for a log so many
tides ago.

So, as you walk around Charleston and experience the
charm, beauty, and hospitality of this elegant Southern City,
Y'all need to come down by the waters edge and say "Hey".
I really like meeting new people
and you can rest assured that
I'll ALWAYS be LOOKING and LISTENING.

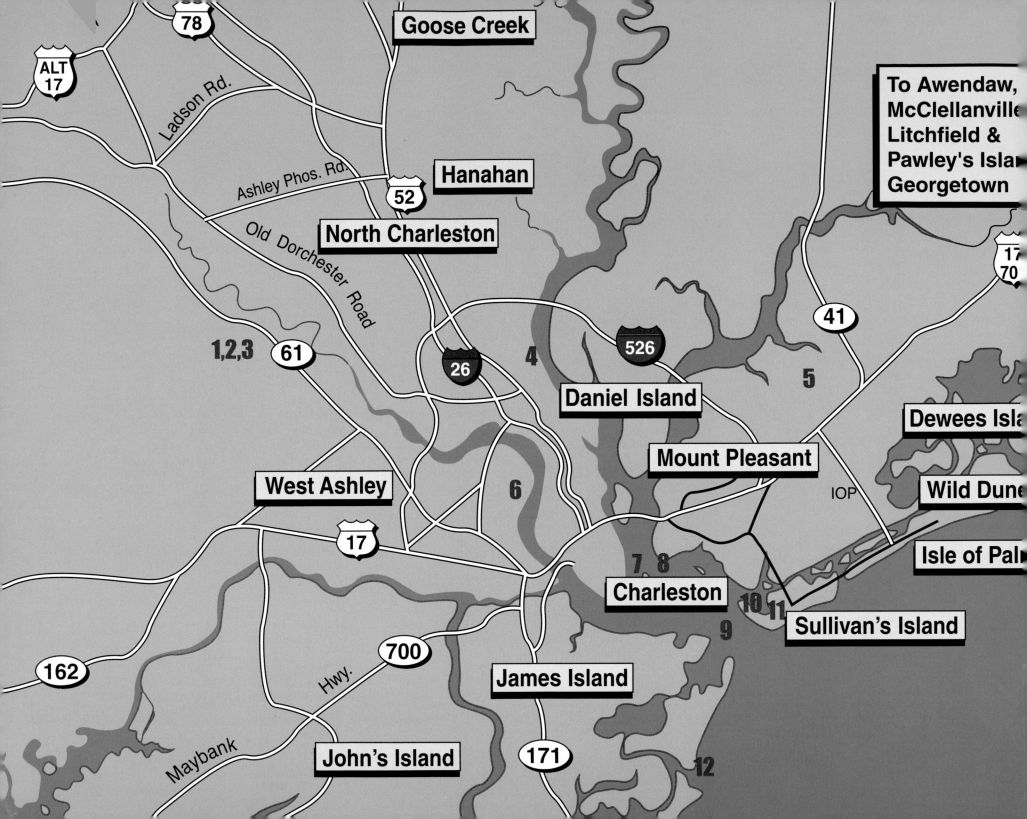

PLUFFER'S CHARLESTON TOUR

1. MIDDLETON PLACE PLANTATION
2. MAGNOLIA PLANTATION
3. DRAYTON HALL PLANTATION
4. H. L. HUNLEY EXHIBIT
5. BOONE HALL PLANTATION
6. CHARLES TOWNE LANDING
7. SOUTH CAROLINA AQUARIUM
8. PATRIOTS POINT
9. FORT SUMTER
10. FORT MOULTRIE
11. SULLIVANS ISLAND LIGHTHOUSE
12. MORRIS ISLAND LIGHTHOUSE

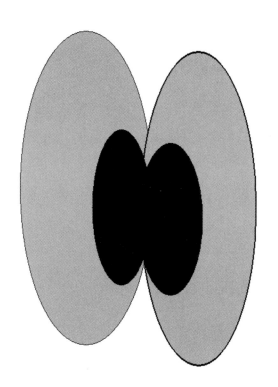

Joseph C. Wilson

I was born and raised in Dayton, Ohio. After graduating from Oakwood High School and a brief encounter with Sinclair College, I decided to join the Navy. It was the Navy that brought me to Pensacola, where I quickly learned that life in the southern latitudes was the life for me.

It was a career in sales that has allowed me to enjoy life in the South and pursue my hobby of boating and sailing. I moved to Charleston from the Gulf Coast 1994. Today, I live aboard my boat "GREEN FLASH" here in Charleston.

I was initially inspired to put this book together to give "Pluffer" an identity, but it has become much more. It was such a pleasure to work with Carol. She is a wonderfully talented artist and her work exceeded all my expectations.

But, I couldn't have done any of this without Charleston. It's such a beautiful City and so prominent in the history of this country. I'm thankful every morning to wake up in such a wonderful place.

Carol Ann Powell

Carol Ann Powell was born and raised in Dartford Kent, England. She credits her artistic father, John Nightingale, for giving her the love of art by teaching her how to draw in childhood. Despite the fact that Carol has had no formal training in painting, she is self-taught from books and using other resources.

Each piece of artwork Carol creates holds some kind of emotion for her. As her paintings evolve, time tends to stand still while she becomes lost in a sea of colors. Once the process is done and the painting is complete, Carol feels that she has left more than just paint on a canvas; she has left a piece of herself.

Carol's paintings for this book were easily inspired because of her love for Charleston. Her children, Alexandra and Courtney, live in England while Carol has resided in Charleston since 1997 with her husband, Phillip, and their two children, Richard and Thomas. Carol thanks her family for all their love and support.